ZION WILLINGHAM

# Found

*First edition*

*This book was professionally typeset on Reedsy.*
*Find out more at reedsy.com*

# Contents

# 1

# Your Joyous Return

# 2

# The Invitation

If you are reading this book as an unsaved person, God is tugging at your heart. Turn to him today.

*2 Peter 3:9*

*The Lord is not slack concerning his promise, as some men count slackness; but is longsuffering to us-ward, not willing that any should perish, but that all should come to repentance.*

The most important act of faith is salvation. God does not want you to perish, but he wants you to come into the salvation that was prepaid for you by Jesus Christ. If you know that you are unsaved, or you are unsure of the status of your salvation, today is the day of salvation.

*John 3:16*

*"For God so loved the world, as to give his only begotten Son; that whosoever believeth in him, may not perish, but may have life everlasting. ... For God so loved the world, that he gave his only Son, that whoever believes in him should not perish but have eternal life."*

*Romans 10:9-10*

*That if thou shalt confess with thy mouth the Lord Jesus, and shalt believe in thine heart that God hath raised him from the dead, thou shalt be saved.*

*10 For with the heart man believeth unto righteousness, and with the mouth, confession is made unto salvation.*

So what will you do? Salvation is yours if you will take it today. Do not make the mistake of listening to an evil spirit of procrastination about this matter.

2 Corinthians 6:2

*For he saith, I have heard thee in a time accepted, and in the day of salvation have I succored thee: behold, now is the accepted time; behold, now is the day of salvation*

Path to Salvation

To repent means three important things.

To turn away from

To change the way you think

To change the way you act.

Repeat this prayer.

Father, in the name of Jesus, I know I am a sinner. I repent of my sins. I need your help to change the way I think and act, as I turn away from my sins. I break all alignment with the Devil and ask you to receive me as your child. I confess you as my Lord and believe you died on the cross and rose again to save my soul. I enter into the Kingdom of God in Jesus' name I pray. Amen.

Salvation is always the most important step. Now You need to be filled with the Holy Ghost

The Holy Spirit has been poured out on all flesh, therefore you can come boldly before the throne to seek this important tool. (Isaiah 44:33) (Hebrews 4:16)

There is a difference between the gift of tongues and the initial indwelling. Think of it as with regular language.  Some people are fluent in several languages, while others only speak one

You can absolutely receive the indwelling of the Holy Spirit instantly at an anointed prayer meeting. On the other hand, you may need to fast and pray.

Even if you are a seasoned Christian, your first utterance may sound a bit like gibberish.  I liken it to children.  They don't come out speaking fluently.  In time, it will change.

Refuse to listen to the Spirit of Unbelief and Doubt. They will almost scream in your ear phrases like. "You are making yourself so that." "It's not real" "It doesn't sound like someone else's." These are all ploys to discourage you and keep you from speaking in tongues. The Bible says that if you "open your mouth he will fill it."(Psalm 81:10)

My suggestion is to create a strong praise and worship environment after a day or so of fasting and prayers. Close your ears to unbelief. Open your mouth and let him fill it with the blessed indwelling of the Holy Spirit.

If you received Salvation or the indwelling of the Holy Spirit, I want to hear about it. Please only post testimonies at parentsarms.com or sanctuaryprayer ministries@wordpress.com.

The only way to truly succeed is to resolve the issue of eternity. I will never tell you that this decision is easy, that it should be taken lightly. I will tell you that when Jesus said, "it is finished," he crossed the finish line with you and me on his shoulders. We were his cross. He didn't give up on us. Never give up on yourself. The race was already won. Join the winning team today.

# 3

# Prayer for Repentance and Mercy From Daniel and the Marine Strongman

Each willing member of the household should openly confess their sins as much as possible. It is important to not interrupt or blame. You must repent before God and move forward! Repentance can be a family affair and individual. Now read the following cry for mercy from Prayer Warrior Daniel:

*"Now, Lord our God, who brought your people out of Egypt with a mighty hand and who made for yourself a name that endures to this day, we have sinned, we have done wrong. 16 Lord, in keeping with all your righteous acts, turn away your anger and your wrath from Jerusalem, your city, your holy hill. Our sins and the iniquities of our ancestors have made Jerusalem and your people an object of scorn to all those around us.*

*17 "Now, our God, hear the prayers and petitions of your servant. For your sake, Lord, look with favor on your sanctuary, our home*

*18 Give ear, our God, and hear; open your eyes and see the desolation of the tabernacle that bears we have dedicated to you. We do not make requests of you because we are righteous, but because of your great mercy.*

*19 Lord, listen! Lord, forgive! Lord, hear and act! For your sake, my God, do not delay, because we, your people, bear your Name."*

Now begin to ask God for mercy. Simply say, Lord have mercy on us. Continue praying for mercy until the presence of the Lord is felt.  I strongly suggest worship music during this process.  Now is the time for open and private confessions.

* This is not the time to yell or argue.  The confessions are to God, for your home! If you suspect that this exercise will do more harm than good, I strongly suggest private confessions or completing this exercise with your Pastor, Christian Counselor, or a mature and trusted Child of God.

*Luke 18:35*

*And hearing the multitude pass by, he asked what it meant. And they told him, that Jesus of Nazareth passeth by. And he cried, saying, Jesus, thou Son of David, have mercy on me.*

Don't leave this potent weapon on the table. Let me give you a real-life story about mercy. I hope it makes you chuckle when you consider the pure irony. You should recognize this story.

*Mark 5:1 (Mercy Personified)*

*And they came over unto the other side of the sea, into the country of the Gadarenes.*

*And when he was come out of the ship, immediately there met him out of the tombs a man with an unclean spirit,*

*Who had his dwelling among the tombs; and no man could bind him, no, not with chains:*

*Because that he had been often bound with fetters and chains, and the chains had been plucked asunder by him, and the fetters broken in pieces: neither could any man tame him.*

*And always, night and day, he was in the mountains, and in the tombs, crying, and cutting himself with stones.*

*But when he saw Jesus afar off, he ran and worshipped him,*

*And cried with a loud voice, and said, What have I to do with thee, Jesus, thou Son of the most high God? I adjure thee by God, that thou torment me not.*

*For he said unto him, Come out of the man, thou unclean spirit.*

*And he asked him, What is thy name? And he answered, saying, My name is Legion: for we are many.*

*And he besought him much that he would not send them away out of the country.*

*Now there was there nigh unto the mountains a great herd of swine feeding.*

*And all the devils besought him, saying, Send us into the swine, that we may enter into them.*

*And forthwith Jesus gave them leave. And the unclean spirits went out, and entered into the swine: and the herd ran violently down a steep place into the sea, (they were about two thousand;) and were choked in the sea.*

This is a story that illustrates just how amazing the mercy of Jesus is to everyone and everything. Let's take a discerning look at this scripture. It not only gives a view of the mercy of Jesus, but the evil marine strongman and his many cohorts gave a very revealing blueprint to answered prayers.

1. Listen for the voice of the Lord.
   Marine Spirit: "But when he saw
   Jesus afar off, he ran"

2. Fall down and worship
   Marine Spirit: worshipped him,

3. Find out the will of God.
   Marine Spirit: And cried with a
   loud voice, and said, What have I to
   do with thee, Jesus, thou Son of the
   most high God?"

4. Humble yourself and make the petition in the name of Jesus
   Marine Spirit: I adjure thee by God,
   that thou torment me not.

5. Be Specific
   Marine Spirit: And he besought
   him much that he would not send
   them away out of the country.

*Now there was there nigh unto the mountains a great herd of swine feeding.*

*And all the devils besought him, saying, Send us into the swine, that we may enter into them.*

So there you have it. An evil confederation of spirits had the insight to worship Jesus and pray to him in the name of God. He did this correctly postured in humility, and his prayer was answered. If an evil troop of marine spirits can have their prayers answered, there is no reason you cannot find your way back to salvation.

4

# Introduction

The original title of this book was, How Did I Get Here, with a subtitle; Finding Your Way Back to God.  The problem with that title was that most people who backslide know, to some level at least, **how** they found themselves in a backslidden state.  The question that plagues many people is **why** did they backslide.  What process in their Christian walk failed?  They often find themselves asking, "How did I get here?"

The backslide is never obvious. The potential for a falling away is so great that the Apostle Paul admonished the saints in

*1 Corinthians 10:12*
   *Wherefore let him that thinketh he standeth take heed lest he fall.*

In other words, standing in the Body of Christ is a deliberate decision. This must be done with an active mind. You must actively decide to be saved each day. You must be aware of your standing. If at any point you become passive about your salvation, you have already begun to backslide.

*1 Corinthians 10:13*
   *There hath no temptation taken you but such as is common to man: but God is*

*faithful, who will not suffer you to be tempted above that ye are able; but will with the temptation also make a way to escape, that ye may be able to bear it.*

It is common to assign blame to various temptations. This is true to a degree. I submit to you that the biggest temptation is the temptation to backslide and, in particular, to shift our spiritual life into autopilot while devoting active mental faculties to other things. The result is the backslide.

Never underestimate how dangerous it is to backslide. It may sound paranoid, but Satan has assigned agents to not only work towards helping you to backslide but to ensure that you never make it back to God.

Let's consider what Jesus told Peter

*Luke 22:31*
   *Simon, Simon, Satan has asked to sift each of you like wheat.*

Let's see verse 32 from different angles

*New International Version*
   *But I have prayed for you, Simon, that your faith will not fail. And when you have* **turned back**, *strengthen your brothers*

*King James Bible*
   *But I have prayed for thee, that thy faith fail not: and when thou art* **converted**, *strengthen thy brethren*

*Good News Translation*
   *News Translation*
   *But I have prayed for you, Simon, that your faith will not fail. And when you* **turn back to me**, *you must strengthen your brothers."*

Each of these translations yields a different view of how Jesus views backsliding. The NIV version uses the term "turn back." The implied statement is that you had to have turned or turned away, to be prompted to turn back. Notice that Jesus did not use language that conveyed walking away, he also did not allude to the fact that the disciples would run away. He used imagery that communicates someone turning their back on someone else.

This situation is so dire that Apostle Peter compared it to a dog returning to his own vomit in 2 Peter 2:22. This is not to rub in your mistake. How could I, when I have been in your shoes? I backslid and it was disastrous.

What if I told you that your backslide may not have been only your fault? I am certain I would sound like an irresponsible Christian who wants to help you find someone to blame for your moral failures. This could not be further from the truth. I only mean to provoke you to take another look at your backslide. Why? The reason is that underlying issues such as witchcraft or demonic oppression often lay seemingly dormant on the surface while secretly working to sabotage you.

These issues must be addressed as you reintegrate yourself into the body of Christ. Make no mistake, get back to Christ first! Then deal with the underlying issues to stay saved. I would be remiss if I did not present salvation to you at this point.

Repeat This Simple Prayer

Father, I cannot save myself, and I cannot keep myself saved. I know that without you, I can never be who I was created to be. I need you. I ask that you will open my eye to receive the ministry in this book. Please help me to change the way I think and act. I thank you for the gift of salvation. Now I pray that you will fill me or increase my yielding to the Holy Ghost so that I will receive the power to fight and overcome every familiar spirit that is laying claim to my life. I confess that I am free and righteous through your blood. In Jesus' name, I pray. Amen.

In this book, we will address some of the reasons for backsliding. What you do as you reintegrate yourself is crucial to your spiritual walk

Now that you are back, let's navigate the road back from backsliding.

# 5

# Welcome Back

You enter into the Wednesday prayer service. You are prepared to pick right up where you left off.  Maybe you were on a board or in a group.  As the announcements are read, you suddenly get the feeling of being an outsider. You look around and see new people occupying the place that you formerly held.

Suddenly you become conscious of the fact that you are returning from backsliding. How many of these people saw you out dressed inappropriately or behaving like a heathen? You understand the mechanics of returning to God, but how do you return to church? Maybe you left the church angry at the leaders. Maybe you were wrong. How do you reacquaint?

First and foremost, stop apologizing. Don't misunderstand me, you should make the necessary apologies <u>once</u>.  You cannot and should not become a professional apologizer.  Meaning that the way some people deal with discomfort is to apologize. God has forgiven you. Pick yourself up. It's time to move forward as a stronger saint. Maybe you were on the usher board, the choir, the women's league, and the cleaning crew. Now you are a different person. You have come back stronger and more genuine than ever. So how about taking your time and joining only one committee, if asked, and doing it well. If you are not asked, don't volunteer during this season.

Pray hard and enjoy the meat of the Word of God. Involve yourself in becoming steadfast in the things of God. Don't be afraid to decline any church activity that will compromise your freedom and rebuilding. You come to church to get more of God. Keep church activities in perspective.

You have not if you ask not. This time, commit to scheduling counseling with your leaders. Make use of the resources available to keep you spiritually healthy. Be more concerned about the Word of God and building than diving back in where you left off in the busyness of the ministry. So how does this look?

Karen was the head of the women's guild. She was a seemingly strong and vibrant member of the church. She served in many areas of the church faithfully for over ten years. Unfortunately, after a strong disagreement with the Pastor's daughter, Karen found herself being rebuked sharply by the Pastor's wife. Out of anger and bewilderment, she stayed home from church in protest.

One Sunday became one month and time ticked on. Karen felt that the Pastor and his wife would certainly miss her contributions. She was shocked when neither the Pastor nor his wife ever contacted her to apologize. Eventually, she tried to attend other churches. She never fit in. In addition, she received several prophetic words to return to her home church.

Time passed and she soon found herself unable to pray. She slowly stopped watching Christian television. Her radio station changed to popular music. She began to redirect her busyness to worldly pursuits.

Seven years later and Karen no longer desired the things of God. It certainly seemed that she might be lost. It was divine providence that found Karen. She attended a play about hell and was convicted. She returned from backsliding. The next Sunday, she found herself sitting in the church that was the scene of her initial backslide.

The Pastor's daughter was busy serving in Karen's old position. The old anger approached Karen, threatening to pull her back out of the church. She found herself face-to-face with the real enemy, unforgiveness.

Karen was determined to overpower the unforgiveness that pulled her out of the church previously. Soon, she was a regular church attendant. This time, when asked to serve on multiple departments, she only committed herself to activities that she could do for the love of God, not the busyness of church.

She was much stronger than she had ever been. The Pastor's wife never apologized, and Karen no longer needed it. Eventually, Karen married a Man of God and found a reward for her faithfulness. As a first lady, she learned from her experiences.

My Analysis

Karen overcame offenses and was blessed for it. I would like to tell you that church hurt will never happen. I would love to tell you that if offenses come, there will always be an acceptable resolution.

At our best, we are redeemed flesh. Nothing should ever separate us from the love of God that is in Christ Jesus. God blessed Karen's humility. Maybe your backslide was not the result of church politics. Whatever the reason, the key to a triumphant return is a change in nature. It is a change in priorities. This may mean seasons of being a "pew-warmer" until God is more important than any position in the church. If anyone can separate you from the love of God, you have gone into idolatry. Read the following scriptures and reflect on the implications:

Romans 8:35-39

Who shall separate us from the love of Christ? shall tribulation, or distress, or persecution, or famine, or nakedness, or peril, or sword? As it is written, For thy sake we are killed all the day long; We are accounted as sheep for the slaughter. Nay, in all these things we are more than conquerors through him that loved us. For I am persuaded, that neither death, nor life, nor angels, nor principalities, nor powers, nor things present, nor things to come, nor height, nor depth, nor any other creature, shall be able to separate us from the love of God, which is in Christ Jesus our Lord.

# 6

# FAQ'S

Book Stuffing?

Why do all of your books have so many scriptures?

Answer

I hope that anywhere you find yourself, especially in warfare, you will be armed with the Word of God and prayers. I want you to be able to use this book to find appropriate scriptures so that you can quickly react when needed.

I need a church

Pray for the Lord to quickly associate you with a ministry. Take your time and when you find a church, be faithful. In the meantime, I invite you to join me on Monday, Wednesday, and Friday for our weekly podcast. In addition, a weekly message is posted on our websites.

Join us on our website at:

https://parentsarms.com

https://zionwillingham.com

Our WordPress:

sanctuaryprayerministries.wordpress.com

Our YouTube Channel: https://tinyurl.com/semfeuht

# 7

# Change Your Palette

I have flirted with veganism and vegetarianism for several years. I love the lifestyle but found myself vacillating back and forth.  One of the greatest lessons I learned from people who successfully embraced and sustained the lifestyle was that the best way to enjoy the lifestyle is to change the way you view food. In other words, people who embark on the lifestyle with the attitude of finding vegetable replacements for the foods they love are often disappointed with the taste of the replacement items. Mind you, some amazing replacement items may even taste better than their animal counterparts. That notwithstanding, a juicy steak is a juicy steak. Jackfruit cannot replace a steak.

On the other hand, if you embark on a vegan or vegetarian diet as a plan to explore new foods and processes. You will find new foods to love and eventually change your palette. This can only happen when you try new foods without the anchoring bias of the foods to which you have become accustomed.  In other words, if you eat eggplant to replace scrambled eggs, the eggplant meal is less likely to be enjoyable than an eggplant dish to enjoy eggplant.

So what does this have to do with returning from backsliding?  Well, you are not trying to change your salvation experience, but return to God with a completely new anointing. You return better and more real because you have something you didn't have before. You have experience. Your backsliding will allow you to not only strengthen yourself but your brethren.

Could this be true? One example of this would be Peter. Take a look:

Peter's Backslide
  Mark 26:33-34

Peter answered and said unto him, Though all men shall be offended because of thee, yet will I never be offended.

Truly, I tell you," Jesus declared, "this very night before the rooster crows, you will deny Me three times."

Peter replied, "Even if I have to die with You, I will never deny You." And all the other disciples said the same thing

Matthew 26:69-75
  Meanwhile, Peter was sitting out in the courtyard, and a servant girl came up to him. "You also were with Jesus the Galilean," she said.

But he denied it before them all: "I do not know what you are talking about."

When Peter had gone out to the gateway, another servant girl saw him and said to the people there, "This man was with Jesus of Nazareth."

And again he denied it with an oath: "I do not know the man!"

After a little while, those standing nearby came up to Peter. "Surely you are one of them," they said, "for your accent gives you away."

At that he began to curse and swear to them, "I do not know the man!"

And immediately a rooster crowed.

Then Peter remembered the Word that Jesus had spoken: "Before the rooster crows, you will deny Me three times." And he went outside and wept bitterly.

We all know that bitter weeping. The moment you realize that you are backslidden. Peter, the recognized leader, had denied Jesus.

Acts 2:14

Then Peter stood up with the Eleven, lifted up his voice, and addressed the crowd: "Men of Judea and all who dwell in Jerusalem, let this be known to you, and listen carefully to my words. These men are not drunk, as you suppose. It is only the third hour of the day!

The same man that denied Jesus before two women boldly addressed the crowd. What happened here? We saw the difference from the Law of Encounter. We will discuss this divine ordinance in future chapters. In the context of palette change, it means to become a new person. In other words, you don't want to return to God as the Christian that you were before backsliding. In other words, you need to truly become a new creature. Maybe you were a regular prayer and fasting machine before you backslid. You don't want to be the prayer and fasting machine that you were before, you want to check your motives and develop a relationship that prompts prayer and fasting by the leading of the Holy Spirit. You will likely pray more and find yourself more fulfilled.

Change your palette. How do you change your palette? The best way is to follow the pattern of Peter and the disciples. You need a real life-shaking encounter with the Holy Spirit. When the presence of the Holy Spirit was manifest in the lives of Peter and the disciples, a change in nature occurred. Suddenly Peter's boldness was buttressed by a real encounter. He no longer prayed out of obedience, he was filled with the power to pray. This power gives holy boldness. This power is the source of power behind Peter's words. This power is the power of the Holy Spirit. Can a person remain saved without the Holy Spirit? My answer is, why in the world would they want to? The Holy Spirit was poured out in all flesh. Therefore, even if you have never spoken one word in tongues, the Holy Spirit can keep you saved through the gospel of Jesus Christ.

Romans 1:16

For I am not ashamed of the gospel of Christ: for it is the power of God unto salvation to every one that believeth; to the Jew first, and also to the Greek.

Hallelujah! The power to return from backsliding rests with power. The power of the Holy Spirit and the power of the gospel of Jesus Christ.

Change your palette. Who told you that you only read the prayer of salvation once. There is a impression that a seasoned saint should read the plan of salvation or the confession to life, once and that's it. I defy anyone to show me this in the Word of God.

*1 Corinthians 15:29-31*

*Else, what shall they do which are baptized for the dead, if the dead rise not at all? why are they then baptized for the dead?*

*30 And why stand we in jeopardy every hour?*

*31 I protest by your rejoicing which I have in Christ Jesus our Lord, I die daily.*

Every day is the right time to consider the gospel. Consider the fact that Paul was an apostle of Jesus Christ, yet he found it necessary to be saved from himself daily. Change the way you see salvation from a ritualistic incantation and repetition, which technically is not even detailed in the Bible, to an encounter-based viewpoint. You read the plan of salvation to know Jesus. You also read the gospels to encounter the Gospel (God Spell), which is the power of salvation. You reflect on the Gospel every day for the power to stay saved.

*Romans 1:16*

*For I am not ashamed of the gospel of Christ: for it is the power of God unto salvation to every one that believeth; to the Jew first, and also to the Greek.*

*Psalm 1:2*

*But his delight is in the law of the LORD, and in his law doth he meditates day and night.*

If King David needed to reflect on the Law of the Lord day and night, how much so are those of us snatched out of hell by the Gospel of Jesus Christ.

These days, simple sermons about salvation are not appealing to the modern saints. Instead, we want deep Rhema. Sadly this generation could easily be the most oppressed in history. Why? It's simple. The Gospel is the power. When we become too deep for the Gospel, we become too deep for the power of salvation. We also leave crucial blessings on the table.

Exercise

Watch the Jesus movie, Passion, or a related title. Change your palette. You are not seeking to make sustained salvation a part of your Christian program, you are seeking to go back on the Gospel road of power and find your way back to God. I will see you in the next chapter.

# 8

# Law of Encounter

The Oxford dictionary defines an encounter as an "unexpected or casual meeting with someone or something." Sorry Oxford, but there is nothing casual about having a real encounter with God. An encounter with God will change your life.

There is an undeniable shifting that comes from basking in the presence of the Holy Spirit. Time with the Holy Spirit will shift your perception.

How do I know?
   It changed me. If you had asked me if I had real salvation, I would have insisted I was a devout Christian. After all, I was better than many people I knew. I read my Bible and prayed somewhat. I was filled with the Holy Spirit. Yet, a divorce and oppression later, I found myself backslidden. Isn't it amazing that the things you swear you will never do, are the things that you do quickly without God?

The moment I found myself staring in the mirror and wondering what happened to my life was the moment that I was preparing for a true encounter. How does a person descend from ministry training to living in sin with what can only be described as a dragon? It didn't happen overnight, as we will discuss in later chapters.

Something did happen to me that changed my life in one hour. It changed the way I see the world. It became the basis of my worldview. It helped me to understand the pure wickedness that was loitering around my family. It was an encounter.

Christianity can take many dimensions for the child of God. I am convinced that the level of effect that the Christian experience has in a person rests heavily on the encounter. The church can be a crutch in many ways. We can bury bad spiritual habits under the guise of worship. It is far too easy to blend in and walk in an appearance of godliness. Unfortunately, this appearance can even fool the person into the belief that they are holy enough. The danger in this is that the backsliding process had already begun in such a person. Any situation in life that takes this person from church will quickly reveal the level of real Christianity that exists within them.

Sunday mornings find homes full of people who no longer attend church or any other kind of ministry. They intend to again, one day. This is the fallacy of religion without relationship and worship without encounter. The encounter is the difference between Saul and Paul. If you have not truly had a complete shift in your nature, then you are missing an encounter.

Blocks to encounter

You are determined to meet God in prayer. You are sitting next to your bed, determined to press through in prayer. You feel dry and distracted. As thoughts race through your head, you struggle to "pray through." After a while, you get up frustrated. If this continues, It's inevitable that eventually, you will stop sitting down to pray. The moment you break communication and fellowship with the Holy Spirit, the backsliding process has begun.

The way to God is not a clearly defined method. Some people believe that they must pray in tongues until they have a breakthrough in the Spirit.

Unfortunately, Satan and his crew are on to that one and will send Beelzebub and even witchcraft chatter to distract your prayers. Instead, there is a path to prayer that I feel is the easiest way for all people. It is the path of absolute unashamed unrepentant desperation. When you are desperate, you will pray in tongues. If that is dry, you will pray in the understanding. Still dry? You will praise, read the Word of God, concentrate on his goodness and mercy, reflect on testimonies while praying. You will do whatever it takes to reach God. Imagine that connecting with God will automatically bring you 50 million dollars. Would you stop trying after one hour or even ten? No! You would keep pressing. You would develop new ways to reach your goal. You will search your scriptures with a fine-toothed comb to ensure you have not missed some word that would connect you to God. Would any stupid chore or worry matter more? You would do this because you feel that 50 million dollars can solve your problems and give you peace. In reality, God can solve your problems and give you peace. Why do we not seek him with the same fervent consistency? One ugly word, unbelief.

The difference between you and Smith Wigglesworth is unbelief. Don't feel bad. The difference between me and Smith Wigglesworth is unbelief. Yet, we also have a difference that puts us at an advantage. This is the ability to purchase books and videos to build the necessary faith. We have resources that simply were not available during the time of Smith Wigglesworth.

Stories of amazing feats performed by this man of God or other generals of God are great faith-building tools to deal a black eye to the sneaky spiritual of unbelief.

If I were to list the single most pronounced cause of backsliding, I would declare that it is unbelief without blinking an eyelid. Why? It's because so much of our backsliding is due to conditioned unbelief.

I coined the term conditioned unbelief. It means a low underlying system and even culture of unbelief, that exists beneath a seemingly strong faith. It can be likened to the dummy cell phones that they sell in the stores.

The phones have the full appearance of active phones. You can pick them up, and they are as heavy as a regular phone. The buttons press in the same fashion as a regular phone. Yet, they are missing the internal components to power the phone. It is empty inside. The difference will quickly present itself in an emergency. Even a disconnected phone can dial out for emergencies, but a dummy phone cannot. It lacks the internal components to dial out

Unbelief can hollow us out in this way. The sneakiness of the unbelief can lie dormant for many years until the right test. The test is not always obviously bad. It can come in the form of a new job that requires working Sunday mornings. It can come in the form of a new romantic interest that does not have any interest in waiting until marriage for sex. It can come in the form of a contract with a company that promotes or markets products that the Bible frowns upon. It can come in the form of new friends who practice different religions and pressure you to visit their worship center. The possibilities for unbelief are endless.

Unbelief is a deadly spirit. This is due to its stealth operation. Like familiar spirits, the spirit of unbelief learns your voice patterns. It then attempts to predictably program its projections into your thought processes.

If I truly believe that Jesus will be back at noon today, would I bother watching the news, yelling at the kids, or even planning my weekend? Absolutely not! I would be busy checking my works to be sure they would stand in the light of the scrutiny of the Lamb of God. I would be out soul-winning. I would care less if they were friends or foes.

I don't believe that Noah was happy to have to cover his ears to overpower the sound of screaming people as they drowned. The culture was wicked. We know which side of Hades these people were headed. They were determined to go. Yet I imagine a tired Noah exhorting these people, in vain to repent. If I told you that a major earth-cleansing event was coming that would see the wicked perish in a like fashion, and the entire body of Christ believed me, businesses would close early. Children would stay home reciting the gospel with careful parents prodding them for belief levels. Borderline and worldly Christians would hop off of their lukewarm seats and get on fire for God.

How could I be so sure of this? My confidence is in the desire of man for self-preservation. If the people of Noah's day had believed that a flood was coming, they would have so intruded into the building of the ark that instead of the size of an aircraft carrier, it would have been the size of ten cities and crammed shoulder-to-shoulder with people. The motivation of these people would not have been the love of God but the desire for self-preservation.

Guess what? God would have saved them. What? Could I be serious? Would God save ungrateful people who only entered the ark to save their own rotten hide? Yes. This is the premise behind salvation. I love the Lord, but God rocked my world when he told me the perfect way to love him is through his Word. Our emotions are fallible, but the Word of God never fails.

The desire for self-preservation was not employed by the people of Noah's day. They died of clinical unbelief. Could this happen again with several billion proclaimed Christians walking the earth? I assure you that it can.

Encounter is more than one of the most powerful tools against unbelief. Encounter is a necessary component of a genuine walk with God. What if I told you that the people of Noah's day couldn't believe due to lack of encounter. They were fully aligned with fallen angels and evil personalities. Their belief was cemented in their experiences. The sad truth is that they believed alright. They believed it too late. The time to get in the ark is never when the door is closed.

So I will return to my previous statement. If we truly knew that Jesus was returning this day at noon, we would beat down the door to get in the ark. We would spend time warning the people to prepare. Unfortunately, we do not operate in constant readiness because we also do not believe. We need an encounter with the Holy Spirit. A prophet of God sings the song, Shake Us Again. We need to be shaken again. It's very simple, if we don't shake ourselves into revival, Satan and his emissaries will gladly attempt to shake us out of the salvation of God.

I recommend finding a quiet place to build an altar. An altar is a place in which we meet God. It needs to be a regular meeting place. This place is your Bethel. This place is the difference between real salvation and people operating in a form of godliness

It is frightening to think that a Jihadist can strap a bomb to their chest and walk in a crowd of people for a God that never died for them. On the other hand, Christians walk in a current of underlying unbelief in the God who gave everything, including his life, for us. The people of Noah's day will have more excuses. Don't wait until Jesus returns to create a Bethel. Build your ark today.

# 9

# Pride to the Side

Pride goes before destruction and a haughty spirit before a fall. I am convinced that if backsliding had a recipe, pride would be a key ingredient. The reason for this is simple. Pride will make you say no when God says yes. Pride will make you begin to use "I Am" statements. Ask Lucifer how great a fall pride can bring. Pride will make you destroy your entire body to save face.

Pride is so potent because it disguises so well. In the previous chapter, Karen had a valid concern, yet pride blinded her to the fact that she risked her everlasting soul to be right. Meanwhile, the person she wanted to punish continued to attend church unphased. Who did she really hurt? Praise God that Karen's story ends well. It is a sad fact that plenty of people like Karen never make it back to Christ. In addition, wonderful growth opportunities can be missed by simply leaving the fold. Thank God that she put her pride to the side and walked into her destiny. How many men and women plan to come back to church one day, only to never make it back. Pride will partner with familiar spirits to convince you that people might laugh or mock you for returning to church after backsliding. My answer is, let them mock! This is your soul and the quality of your life. I will rest this scripture:

Romans 8:35-39

Who shall separate us from the love of Christ? shall tribulation, or distress, or persecution, or famine, or nakedness, or peril, or sword? As it is written, For thy sake we are killed all the day long; We are accounted as sheep for the slaughter. Nay, in all these things we are more than conquerors through him that loved us. For I am persuaded, that neither death, nor life, nor angels, nor principalities, nor powers, nor things present, nor things to come, nor height, nor depth, nor any other creature, shall be able to separate us from the love of God, which is in Christ Jesus our Lord.

People and their mouths do not have the authority to separate you from the love of God unless you let them. Pride will strip you of your power. Even if you have no one to be concerned about in the persecution arena, you must address the pride that caused the backslide in the first place. Did you get too busy for God? Were you offended by God or someone else? Did someone injure you? Whatever the reason, a quick departure from pride is critical to maintaining your salvation. These are the foxes that spoil the vine. We don't take issues like unbelief and pride seriously, therefore they work uninterrupted. At the end of this book, you will find a journal. I suggest keeping track of your reactions. What triggered them? Let's revisit our third-grade English and gather a definition. There are several definitions of pride, but the one to watch is "consciousness of one's own dignity."

When you are conscious of it, you will take steps to protect it. When you are conscious of your arms, you take steps to protect them. Faith relies on the conscious belief that God will protect our dignity. Pride will not allow us to trust God with our dignity.

Pride is a work of the flesh and a spirit. I often quote Watchman Nee in my declaration of sympathy with the Holy Spirit. A fall from the grace of God into backsliding is illustrative of some sympathy with the Spirit of Pride. Ask the Holy Ghost to reveal where you are sympathizing with the Spirit of Pride.

The Herald Magazine gave the following examples of pride:

"● Self-righteous: "I don't need the grace of God." Do you spend more time thinking about yourself than about God or about other people?

● Ego and confidence: Why do I have to always voice my opinions to others? Do I speak constantly without listening?

● Trial of comparison: Do I compare myself with others often, judging myself favorably?

● Do I take pleasure in something by which I measure my own self-worth along the lines of looks, intelligence, or ability?

● Wealth or high status: Do I try to make sure that others are aware of my personal gifts or possessions?

● Contentment: Do I think I deserve more of this world's good things than other people do?

● Will I get what I want: Am I willing to pursue my selfish goals even if it means others are hurt in the process?

● Holier than thou: Do I think God must be pleased with me because of how ethical or religious I am?

● Self sufficient: Do I ever think I do not really need God or other people?" (herald-magazine.org, 2021)

Take an honest assessment. Problems such as lust, lying, and even anger are easy to detect. Take the time to find the pride that prompted your backslide. This is where your pride will be tested. I urge you that consult with your leaders for a real assessment of this issue. I preface this with the statement that you must want to stay saved worse than you want to save face. It's not easy to hear that we are prideful, but it is worse to hear the words "depart from me" as you are standing before God.  Perspective is everything.  See you in the next chapter.

# 10

# The Fall of the Wallflower

No one noticed that you have backslidden because you are basically hidden. You are the person who attends church every Sunday, yet have never heard the closing prayer. Why? Because you raise your index finger and gently make your way to the door within ten minutes of the close of the sermon. You might pay tithes and offerings, but nobody can ever remember your name without struggling. The Wallflower is not the person who is a caregiver or has responsibilities that would prompt them to decline most activities within a church, a ministry, or even witnessing. The Wallflower is simply non-committal. This is not meant as a rebuke. The Wallflower has decided that church is a part of their life in the same fashion as a club. They fit it in, and it makes things look nice. That is until life gets ugly. Suddenly the non-committal wallflower becomes the backslider. Unfortunately, because of this nature, no one even notices that the person no longer attends. Even if they do, the wallflower refuses to make the sort of connections that would allow someone into their ashes.

I understand that not everyone is a social butterfly, but truly the non-committal attitude is simply not wanting to be held responsible. There may be many reasons, yet the most harmful reason was a refusal to commit to a certain church or be held accountable for appearing in church regularly. Now that you are finding your way back from backsliding, please pick a ministry or several ministries to commit to. In other words, you may be a partner in one ministry and attend another ministry. You may catch all messages and even sow into an online or television ministry while regularly attending and supporting your church. Maybe you are lead to visit a prayer ministry each evening. Do it. Find out what resources they are offering and take advantage of them. Whatever you take on to do, stick with it.

Most importantly, get counseling from spiritual leaders in this ministry and take on some responsibility for God. Some ministries, like Sanctuary Prayer Ministries, are not fashioned like typical ministries. Speak with the leader of the ministry to discover where you can best be of service. I can guarantee that there is plenty to do.

The accountability that makes you uncomfortable is a safety net that will keep you from slipping through the cracks. The bible says that in the multitude of counselors, there is safety. (Proverbs 11:14)

## What about church hurt

Church hurt has created more wallflowers than any other device of the devil. I discussed some church hurts in previous chapters. Let me assure you that the solution for dealing with church hurt is not to quit church altogether. My controversial statement is that not every church is for everyone. I do not believe that a person needs to force themselves to submit to a ministry that makes them lament in their walk for God. Take your time and find the right ministry. Once you receive the release to join from the Holy Ghost, work like someone who was snatched out of hell because you were.

## My Testimony

I love the church. Yet I backslid, fell into sin, fell into a viper's nest, and barely made it back to God. No, I wasn't a wallflower, but I also did not attend church. God gave me a ministry that is designed for people who feel unwelcome or unable to attend the typical church. We seek to minister to people with hypervigilance, trauma, and oppression of all types. Don't think for one minute that I do not understand how you feel. That notwithstanding, I am more concerned with your soul. You must do something. Your spiritual man requires more food and water than your physical man. You must read the Word of God and receive word somehow. If you cannot find it somewhere, please go online. Find some way to connect with the body and get under an anointing. Find Christian people to associate with. Change your reading to at least one Christian book per month. Change your television patterns. This is the way to ensure you stay standing. See you in the next t chapter.

# 11

# Satan's Sneaky Schemes

Why do some people seem to be permanent travelers on the road back from backsliding? They leave the church, they come back. In no time, they are gone again. They may have done this for several years. I can remember being a brand new saint and observing several people who had been in the church before I came. Yet, they would come and go so often that it always seemed like they never grew. I liken it to starting a bicycle marathon and looking over to see a few people on stationary bikes. Each time you lap, they are always there peddling in the same place. This is the occupational hazard of backsliding. Some people stop going to church but continue to read their Bible and pray. They negotiate ways to introduce the Word of God into their lives. These people may continue to grow. Unfortunately, it is far more common for people to leave a church, only to settle into a godless existence until something happens or God pricks their hearts.

Satan is very interested in backsliders. He loves serial backsliders and will work diligently to ensure a backslidden person never makes it back to God. He will send all of the old distractions and temptations. He will go above and beyond to raise the appeal of these things. He will make you tired during prayer time or church. He will frustrate you in the place of prayer. He will send energy-draining familiar spirits to make you tired before church. He might cause some sort of mechanical malfunction on your vehicle to delay your service. He will send his familiar and other spirits to criticize your clothing with the hope that you will simply decide not to go to church. He will create a situation on your job that will cause you to need to work during church time. He will even ensure that you get a coveted promotion that will interrupt your spiritual responsibilities.

These are Satan's sneaky tricks. The goal is to redirect your attention away from God and back onto something else. He pulls these tricks on everybody, but it seems that the attack against backslidden people comes at a greater frequency. I urge you to read the scriptures I listed in the scripture section and pray the Blood of Jesus. I quoted Dr. Cindy Trimm's book, The Rules of Engagement, in an earlier chapter. I would like to complete that quote. She said that "Our warfare is not with human beings but with the devil and his demons, who propagate doctrines of devils, heresies, Luciferian ideologies, satanic philosophies, and diabolical imagery. Satan attempts to defeat us with strategy and deceit through well-laid plans and deliberate deceptions and manipulation. When he speaks to our minds in an attempt to derail us from following a path that leads to the fulfillment of purpose and destiny: (Trimm, 2008)

A false sense of security could be the reason so many people are leveled by the satanic onslaught that they experience on the road back from backsliding. Let's look at this a bit more in the scriptures.

The Parable of the Sower Explained
(Mark 4:13–20; Luke 8:11–15)
*"18 Consider, then, the parable of the sower: 19 When anyone hears the message of the kingdom but does not understand it, the evil one comes and snatches away what was sown in his heart. This is the seed sownd along the path.*

**20 The seed sown on rocky ground is the one who hears the word and at once receives it with joy. 21But since he has no root, he remains for only a season. When trouble or persecution comes because of the word, he quickly falls away.**

*(Initial Backslider)*

**22 The seed sown among the thorns is the one who hears the word, but the worries of this life and the deceitfulness of wealth choke the word, and it becomes unfruitful. (Returning Backslider)**

*23 But the seed sown on good soil is the one who hears the word and understands it. He indeed bears fruit and produces a crop—a hundredfold, sixtyfold, or thirtyfold."*

The return to salvation is warfare. Maintaining salvation is warfare. Growing in God is warfare. You must be prepared to fight. You can defeat the devil and reach your destination in God. When you return, it is at that point you can help/strengthen others traveling the road back from backsliding with the Word of God and prayer.

Luke 22:32

But I have prayed for thee, that thy faith fail not; and when thou art converted, strengthen thy brethren."

I couldn't help but notice that Jesus did not consider Peter's backsliding a failure. He mentioned that the conditions for a failure would be a failure to return. In other words, Peter blew it, yet Jesus did not consider it a failure. Instead, it seemed to be a part of the process that would introduce the church to the biggest blessing we could ever receive aside from the sacrifice of Jesus Christ. This blessing is the person of the Holy Ghost.

See you in the next chapter.

# 12

# Strength to Stand

You came back! Praise the Lord. You are so excited! This excitement is short-lived as the onslaught from the devil begins. The major attacks usually come from three places

Strongholds- In her book, The Rules of Engagement, Cindy Trimm defined strongholds (ochuroma) as "A pattern and idea that governs individuals, nations, and communities. They are mindsets, thought patterns, and processes that cause people to act, react, and respond in a particular manner contrary to the ways of God, and a godly mindset."(Trimm, 2008)

Temptations- Food and sex are not the only temptations. Every negative emotion has the potential to be a temptation. For example, you fell into sexual sin while backslidden. You have come back to God. Now you receive a text that the woman you slept with is pregnant. You planned to shut the door on this illicit relationship, as you know that this woman was not the will of God for your life. You are afraid. You hear a voice exhorting you to block the woman's telephone number and forget about God, the woman, and the baby.

Accusation- I will include a prayer of renunciation against accusation from my book, Mad As Hell. Satan lives to let the wind out of our sails with accusations. You are floating on air, joyful that you have reconciled with God. Suddenly a voice speaks to you and reminds you of the bad choices that you made while backslidden. If that doesn't work, he will send somebody to play the time of Satanic recall and reply. Even if the comments are presented innocently.

What do you do when Satan threatens to kick your newly standing legs out from under you. When the unrelenting pressure of strongholds, temptations, and accusations seem entirely too much to bear. When Satan puts on his identity as the storm god Baal and unleashes storms against your life. Add to it the fact that nobody told you that these attacks would be sent against you when you were initially saved. They forgot to mention that Satan hates to lose. When you came back to God, he took it personally. So the sudden warfare should be no surprise.

Let me put this in perspective for you. Peter fell flat on his face. He did it publicly. Yet when he returned and had an encounter with the Holy Spirit, his shadow was so electrified with raw power that people were healed by his shadow as he walked by.

Satan will sift your new state to try to make you backside again. He will test you to see if you are sure about the faith that you claim. If he senses any doubt, he will capitalize. Find a saint, read a book, seek pastoral counseling, crawl, scratch, kick, FIGHT! You fail to fight when you fail to believe the Bible when it describes the walk of the saint as warfare. You win when you put on the full armor of God

*Ephesians 6:10-18*

*Finally, my brethren, be strong in the Lord, and in the power of his might.*

*11 Put on the whole armour of God, that ye may be able to stand against the wiles of the devil.*

*12 For we wrestle not against flesh and blood, but against principalities, against powers, against the rulers of the darkness of this world, against spiritual wickedness*

*in high places.*

*13 Wherefore take unto you the whole armour of God, that ye may be able to withstand in the evil day and having done all, to stand.*

*14 Stand therefore, having your loins girt about with truth, and having on the breastplate of righteousness;*

*15 And your feet shod with the preparation of the gospel of peace;*

*16 Above all, taking the shield of faith, wherewith ye shall be able to quench all the fiery darts of the wicked.*

*17 And take the helmet of salvation, and the sword of the Spirit, which is the word of God:*

*18 Praying always with all prayer and supplication in the Spirit, and watching thereunto with all perseverance and supplication for all saints;*

Pray however you have to. Read your Bible militantly. Fast as much as you can, in the way that works between you and God. The strength to stand is encoded in the previous scripture.

*Wherefore take unto you the whole armor of God, that ye may be able to withstand in the evil day, and **having done all, to stand. 14 Stand, therefore,***

Nobody said that tears could not stream down your eyes as you stand. Stand anyway. Goliath, Sennacherib, and Satan all spent forty days and nights harassing the people of God. An enemy does not show up for forty days and nights if the force he is busy tormenting is spiritually empty. In each case, the enemy wanted to break the spirit of the people he was attacking. He used the power of repetition to attempt to condition fear into his targets. Although each battle was won differently, the stand was the same. The intervention of God was undeniable.  The outcome was unexplainable.  Ultimately, only God could take the glory for every victory. Only God could defeat these giants. Likewise, God can defeat your giants. I will see you in the next chapter.

43

# 13

# Accusations of the Devil

This chapter was taken from my book, Mad As Hell.

The word Satan means accuser. This is a job description and not the actual name of the entity terrorizing the world. He fell and will ultimately spend an eternity in the Lake of Fire. We have all fallen in sin and come short of the glory of God, so Jesus came to free us from the Law of Sin and Death. Satan feels that this is terribly unfair. Satan, of course, conveniently leaves out the role that he and his Kingdom play in all of the sins that he constantly accuses us of committing.

When you yield to these accusations about your past, the enemies immediately want to make you depressed. If you become depressed, it opens the door to further demonization. It's not what you did but who you are that determines whether you will spend an eternity in hell. That being said, Jesus told the cripple to go and sin no more lest some worse evil comes upon him. (John 5:14)

A preacher said that Satan keeps a running file of every sin he influences you to commit. He then uses that file to accuse you and form attacks against your life. This reminds me of the movies in which the main character is being blackmailed by an antagonist. The demands of the antagonist continue to grow as the movie progresses. Eventually, the main character becomes fed-up with the extortion and blackmail of the antagonist, and they ultimately admit what they did. The power is taken away from the antagonist. God has given you a path of confession and deliverance. Read your Bible! Don't let any human or spirit, other than the Holy Spirit, reroute your deliverance process to make themselves a gatekeeper of your freedom.

God did not ordain Satan or the Kingdom Of Darkness to be your judge, jury, and executioner! If you are wrong, he can certainly convict you without condemning you. Conviction simply means that he tells you that you are wrong. He may even show you. Saints, this is not ideal. Unfortunately, the conscience of some people is so hard that God has to cut them out of his presence. The judgment of God is a fearful thing. Keep it in the right priority and refuse any fallen personality the right to bind you or keep you in bondage.

On the other hand, your abusers have no right to abuse and torment anyone else, with the plan to turn God's grace into lasciviousness. The power that makes you behave this way is a demon and needs to be cast out! God does love everybody, but hell is enlarging itself daily, and if you enter into eternity in this way, hellfire will be your portion.

For everyone else, struggling with accusations about your past. Especially if it is something that the Bible clearly says you can be forgiven for, know that it is demonic. God did not leave the responsibility of the judgment of your life in the hand of Satan or any evil spirit.

Pray This Way

I address you directly you evil spirit. I first confess anything you are rightfully accusing me of. I repent to Jesus. I not only turn away from it, but I also change the way I think and act. "I speak that any spirits that would loiter around to reintroduce this sin are bound in chains and cast out.

Satan, the Lord rebuke you today. I renounce my past, and I press forward in

Christ Jesus. Jesus, I pray that you will annihilate and eradicate every ounce of legal right through past sins as I press towards a newness in life. I recover myself and any fragmented parts as a result of this sin. I shut every door that was opened through this sin and command the spirits that entered in to be evacuated immediately.

I address you accusing spirits now, and I bind you by the authority of Jesus Christ and declare the word which says that "*There is* therefore now no condemnation to them which are in Christ Jesus, who walk not after the flesh, but after the Spirit." (Romans 8:1)

Now Heavenly Father, I pray that by your right arm, you will cause all accusing spirits to drown in the sea of forgetfulness, where you buried my past sins and transgressions. In Jesus' name, I pray, Amen.

Now read the following scriptures aloud. Place your name and that of your loved ones in the blanks.

Zechariah 3:1-5
    Then I or/and
    _______ [A] was standing before the angel of the Lord, and Satan[a][B] standing at my or _________ right side to accuse me or _______ 2 The Lord said to Satan, "The Lord rebuke you,[C] Satan! The Lord, who has chosen[D] Jerusalem, rebuke you! Is not this man/woman/child a burning stick[E] snatched from the fire?"[F]

3 Now I and/or _________ was dressed in filthy clothes as I/we or _________ stood before the angel. 4 The angel said to those who were standing before _______, "Take off _________ filthy clothes."

Then he said to _________, "See, I have taken away your sin,[G] and I will put fine garments[H] on you."

Then I said, "Put a clean turban[(I)] on _________ head." So they put a clean turban on _______ head and clothed _______, while the angel of the Lord stood by.

Father, in the name of Jesus, I thank you for removing all corrupt, stained, defiled, and filthy garments from my life. I release every evil spirit that is attached to me as a result of Satan's accusations and spiritual defilement.

I recover every good thing that was blocked, hindered, exchanged, or stolen from my life. As Joshua was dressed as royalty in the presence of the Angel of the Lord, so may I/we or _______ receive a one-hundred fold return of glory, virtues, stars, and destiny. In Jesus' name, I pray. Amen.

<u>Now seal these declarations with scripture</u>

(Isaiah 49:24-26
  Shall the prey be taken from the mighty, or the lawful captive delivered?

[25] But thus saith the Lord, Even the captives of the mighty shall be taken away, and the prey of the terrible shall be delivered: for I will contend with him that contendeth with thee, and I will save thy children.

[26] And I will feed them that oppress thee with their own flesh; and they shall be drunken with their own blood, as with sweet wine: and all flesh shall know that I the Lord am thy Saviour and thy Redeemer, the mighty One of Jacob.

Now you have to truly receive this. Do not consider this exercise complete until you are certain about your confession.

If you continue to hear accusing voices, have accusing thoughts, or you are being attacked by an evil spirit of Recall and Replay. Bind the Spirit of Recall and Replay and any other spirit that the Holy Ghost reveals to you. Loose the spirits of a sound mind, such as Perfect Peace. If the attacks persist after you complete this book, consider purchasing the Self-Deliverance Manual.

<u>Perspective</u>

If the enemy is busy talking about your past, it means he is not aligned with your present. Don't look back, think back, or reflect back. Time does not go back.

Philippians 3:13-15

Brethren, I count not myself to have apprehended: but this one **thing** I do, **forgetting those things which are behind**, and reaching forth unto **those things** which are before, 14. I press toward the mark for the prize of the high calling of God in Christ Jesus.

Have you ever tried to push something forward while looking backward? Suffice to say that your effort will not be at its best. Resolve yourself to press forward. Allow yourself to bask in not only the beautiful forgiveness of God but the resolute and consistent forgiveness of yourself.

Your past does not have authority over you "are" unless you give it to it. There are plenty of reasons that you might, but ultimately, the authority over "were" is in the automatic jurisdiction of your past. Your future is in the hands of God. Therefore, press in the present. When you feel secure in this matter, I will see you in the next chapter.

# 14

# The Blood of Jesus

**<u>Blood of Jesus</u>**

Leviticus 17:10-12

I stand in my authority as a blood-bought, covenanted child of God, and I plead the blood of Jesus on anything that does not look like God in my life.

**<u>Your Right of Access (Read Out Loud)</u>**

I assert that the following consideration has been tendered for my right, which I henceforth assert:

Isaiah 53:5

**But he was wounded for our transgressions**,

* You cannot claim my forgiven past as a legal right of entry.

**he was bruised for our iniquities:**

*You cannot claim my forgiven past mindset as a legal right of entry.

**the chastisement of our peace was upon him;**

*Jesus took the psychological warfare so that my mind would be sound. (2 Timothy 1:7)

**and with his stripes, we are healed**
  * I have a right to healing and good health. It was already prepaid.


References Scriptures
  1 John 6-8
  Hebrews 10:18
  Hebrews 12:23-25
  Hebrews 13:19-21
  Revelation 1:5
  1 John 1:7


<u>Plead The Blood of Jesus</u>
  I receive the mercy of God.  Now, as I plead the blood of Jesus, I receive deliverance in the name of Jesus Christ.

I plead the blood of Jesus over the air inside, outside, over, under, and around me.

I plead the blood of Jesus over my home, vehicle, and every structure.

I plead the blood of Jesus over my soul. (mind, will, and emotions)

I plead the blood of Jesus over my family.  Husband, wife, children, and extended family and friends.

I plead the blood of Jesus over my finances.

I plead the blood of Jesus over my neighborhood.

I plead the blood of Jesus over my community.

Declarations

The blood of Jesus frees me from the Law of Sin and Death.

I am alive by the blood of Jesus

The blood of Jesus empowers me with creation power.

The blood of Jesus has healed my finances, my body, my home, my loved ones. Wherever it is applied, it has already healed.

I am a new creature by the blood of Jesus.

I am made new by the blood of Jesus.

I was lame, blind, broken, and torn down in sin. I can now see by the blood of Jesus. I leap with hinds feet by the blood of Jesus. I am made whole by the blood of Jesus. My broken heart is bound by the blood of Jesus. I am a new creature in the blood of Jesus.

# 15

# References


https://herald-magazine.com/2016/11/01/overcoming-pride/amp/

# 16

# Reference Scriptures

# 17

# Faith Scriptures

Faith comes by hearing the Word of God. Be sure to really hear these scriptures. God takes faith very seriously. (Romans 14:23) (Hebrews 11:6) Have faith that God can rebuild your ruins. Have faith in his love for you.

Matthew 8:26

And he saith unto them, Why are ye fearful, O ye of little faith? Then he arose and rebuked the winds and the sea, and there was a great calm.

1 Thessalonians 3:10

Night and day praying exceedingly that we might see your face, and might perfect that which is lacking in your faith

Colossians 2:7

Rooted and built up in him, established in the faith, as ye have been taught, abounding therein with thanksgiving

Ephesians 3:12

2 In whom we have boldness and access with confidence by the faith of him.

Ephesians 3:23

But before faith came, we were kept under the law, shut up unto the faith which should afterwards be revealed.

Ephesians 6:16

Above all, taking the shield of faith, wherewith ye shall be able to quench all the fiery darts of the wicked.

2 Corinthians 5:7

(For we walk by faith, not by sight:)

Romans 4:5

But to him that worketh not, but believeth on him that justifieth the ungodly, his faith is counted for righteousness

Romans 1:17

For therein is the righteousness of God revealed from faith to faith: as it is written, The just shall live by faith.

Romans 3:21-25

22 Even the righteousness of God which is by faith of Jesus Christ unto all and upon all them that believe: for there is no difference:

23 For all have sinned, and come short of the glory of God;

24 Being justified freely by his grace through the redemption that is in Christ Jesus:

25 Whom God hath set forth to be a propitiation through faith in his blood, to declare his righteousness for the remission of past sins, through the forbearance of God;

Mark 11:22

And Jesus answering saith unto them, Have faith in God

You can win!

2 Thessalonians 5:8

But let us, who are of the day, be sober, putting on the breastplate of faith and love; and for an helmet, the hope of salvation.

Matthew 17:20

And Jesus said unto them, Because of your unbelief: for verily I say unto you, If ye have faith as a grain of mustard seed, ye shall say unto this mountain, Remove hence to yonder place; and it shall remove; and nothing shall be impossible unto you.

Acts 3:16

And his name through faith in his name hath made this man strong, whom ye see and know: yea, the faith which is by him hath given him this perfect soundness in the presence of you all.

Matthew 21:21

Luke 17:6

Jesus answered and said unto them, Verily I say unto you, If ye have faith, and doubt not, ye shall not only do this which is done to the fig tree, but also if ye shall say unto this mountain, Be thou removed, and be thou cast into the sea; it shall be done.

Galatians 2:16

Knowing that a man is not justified by the works of the law, but by the faith of Jesus Christ, even we have believed in Jesus Christ, that we might be justified by the faith of Christ, and not by the works of the law: for by the works of the law shall no flesh be justified

Galatians 3:11

But that no man is justified by the law in the sight of God, it is evident: for, The just shall live by faith.

Romans 9:30

What shall we say then?  That the Gentiles, which followed not after righteousness, have attained to righteousness, even the righteousness which is of faith

Your faith, your victory. No faith, no victory. It's just that simple. This seems overly simplified.  It is not meant to be.  Faith is a very complex topic that is based on the reading and integration of the Word of God.  The more you look like the Word illustrated in John 1:1-5, the more faith you will have and the more victories you will have. The Bible laid out some formulas that are beneficial to learn.

Hope + Action = Faith
   (Hebrews 11:1)

Word of God+ Hearing+You= Faith (Romans 10:17)

Faith + you= The help of God
   (Mark 9:23)

You- Faith= No help from God
   (James 1:8)

Faith - Work= 0
   (James 2:26)

# 18

# Fear Scriptures

The opposite of love is fear. The Spirit of Fear is a major driving spirit. It works like the Holy Ghost to cover all flesh. Fear is an evil enemy. I will discuss fear in greater detail in my next book, Trigger Warning. Perfect Love is Jesus. Let him cast out all of your fears.

1 John 4:18

There is no fear in love; but perfect love casteth out fear: because fear hath torment. He that feareth is not made perfect in love.

Genesis 26:24

And the Lord appeared unto him the same night, and said, I am the God of Abraham thy father: fear not, for I am with thee, and will bless thee, and multiply thy seed for my servant Abraham's sake.

Exodus 1:21

And it came to pass, because the midwives feared God, that he made them houses

Exodus 14:13

And Moses said unto the people, Fear ye not, stand still, and see the salvation of the Lord, which he will shew to you to day: for the Egyptians whom ye have seen to day, ye shall see them again no more for ever

Exodus 15:11

Who is like unto thee, O Lord, among the gods? who is like thee, glorious in holiness, fearful in praises, doing wonders

Deuteronomy 3:22

Ye shall not fear them: for the Lord your God he shall fight for you

Deuteronomy 31:6

Be strong and of a good courage, fear not, nor be afraid of them: for the Lord thy God, he it is that doth go with thee; he will not fail thee, nor forsake thee.

2 Kings 6:16

And he answered, Fear not: for they that be with us are more than they that be with them

2 Kings 17:39

But the Lord your God ye shall fear; and he shall deliver you out of the hand of all your enemies

2 Chronicles 20:17

Ye shall not need to fight in this battle: set yourselves, stand ye still, and see the salvation of the Lord with you, O Judah and Jerusalem: fear not, nor be dismayed; to morrow go out against them: for the Lord will be with you

Job 28:28

And unto man he said, Behold, the fear of the Lord, that is wisdom; and to depart from evil is understanding

Psalm 2:11

Serve the Lord with fear, and rejoice with trembling

Psalm 19:9

The fear of the Lord is clean, enduring for ever: the judgments of the Lord are true and righteous altogether

Psalm 23:4

Yea, though I walk through the valley of the shadow of death, I will fear no evil: for thou art with me; thy rod and thy staff they comfort me.

Psalm 25:12

What man is he that feareth the Lord? him shall he teach in the way that he shall choose.

Psalm 25:14

The secret of the Lord is with them that fear him; and he will shew them his covenant.

Psalm 27:1

The Lord is my light and my salvation; whom shall I fear? the Lord is the strength of my life; of whom shall I be afraid?

Psalm 27:3

Though an host should encamp against me, my heart shall not fear: though war should rise against me, in this will I be confident.

Psalm 31:19

Oh how great is thy goodness, which thou hast laid up for them that fear thee; which thou hast wrought for them that trust in thee before the sons of men!

Psalm 33:8

Let all the earth fear the Lord: let all the inhabitants of the world stand in awe of him.

Psalm 33:18

Behold, the eye of the Lord is upon them that fear him, upon them that hope in his mercy;

Psalm 34:4

I sought the Lord, and he heard me, and delivered me from all my fears.

Psalm 34:7

The angel of the Lord encampeth round about them that fear him, and delivereth them.

Psalm 34:9

O fear the Lord, ye his saints: for there is no want to them that fear him.

Psalm 34:11

Come, ye children, hearken unto me: I will teach you the fear of the Lord.

Psalm 36:1

The transgression of the wicked saith within my heart, that there is no fear of God before his eyes.

Psalm 40:3

And he hath put a new song in my mouth, even praise unto our God: many shall see it, and fear, and shall trust in the Lord.

Psalm 46:2

Therefore will not we fear, though the earth be removed, and though the mountains be carried into the midst of the sea;

Psalm 48:6

Fear took hold upon them there, and pain, as of a woman in travail.

Psalm 49:5

Wherefore should I fear in the days of evil, when the iniquity of my heels shall compass me about?

Psalm 56:4

In God I will praise his word, in God I have put my trust; I will not fear what flesh can do unto me.

Psalm 60:4

Thou hast given a banner to them that fear thee, that it may be displayed because of the truth. Selah.

Psalm 85:9

Surely his salvation is nigh them that fear him; that glory may dwell in our land.

Psalm 90:11

Who knoweth the power of thine anger? even according to thy fear, so is thy wrath.

Psalm 96:4

For the Lord is great, and greatly to be praised: he is to be feared above all gods.

Psalm 96:9

O worship the Lord in the beauty of holiness: fear before him, all the earth.

Psalm 102:15

So the heathen shall fear the name of the Lord, and all the kings of the earth thy glory.

Psalm 103:11

For as the heaven is high above the earth, so great is his mercy toward them that fear him.

Psalm 103:13

Like as a father pitieth his children, so the Lord pitieth them that fear him.

Psalm 103:17

But the mercy of the Lord is from everlasting to everlasting upon them that fear him, and his righteousness unto children's children;

Psalm 111:10

The fear of the Lord is the beginning of wisdom: a good understanding have all they that do his commandments: his praise endureth for ever.

Psalm 112:1

Praise ye the Lord. Blessed is the man that feareth the Lord, that delighteth greatly in his commandments.

Psalm 115:11

Ye that fear the Lord, trust in the Lord: he is their help and their shield.

Psalm 115:13

He will bless them that fear the Lord, both small and great.

Psalm 118:4

Let them now that fear the Lord say, that his mercy endureth for ever.

Psalm 118:6

The Lord is on my side; I will not fear: what can man do unto me?

Psalm 119:38

Stablish thy word unto thy servant, who is devoted to thy fear.

Psalm 128:1

Blessed is every one that feareth the Lord; that walketh in his ways.

Psalm 128:4

Behold, that thus shall the man be blessed that feareth the Lord.

Psalm 139:14

I will praise thee; for I am fearfully and wonderfully made: marvellous are thy works; and that my soul knoweth right well.

Psalm 145:19

He will fulfil the desire of them that fear him: he also will hear their cry, and will save them.

Psalm 147:11

The Lord taketh pleasure in them that fear him, in those that hope in his mercy.

Proverbs 1:7

The fear of the Lord is the beginning of knowledge: but fools despise wisdom and instruction.

Proverbs 1:33

But whoso hearkeneth unto me shall dwell safely, and shall be quiet from fear of evil.

Proverbs 2:5

Then shalt thou understand the fear of the Lord, and find the knowledge of God.

Proverbs 3:7

Be not wise in thine own eyes: fear the Lord, and depart from evil.

Proverbs 3:25

Be not afraid of sudden fear, neither of the desolation of the wicked, when it cometh.

Proverbs 8:13

The fear of the Lord is to hate evil: pride, and arrogancy, and the evil way, and the froward mouth, do I hate.

Proverbs 9:10

The fear of the Lord is the beginning of wisdom: and the knowledge of the holy is understanding.

Proverbs 10:24

The fear of the wicked, it shall come upon him: but the desire of the righteous shall be granted.

Proverbs 10:27

The fear of the Lord prolongeth days: but the years of the wicked shall be shortened.

Proverbs 13:13

Whoso despiseth the word shall be destroyed: but he that feareth the commandment shall be rewarded.

Proverbs 14:2

He that walketh in his uprightness feareth the Lord: but he that is perverse in his ways despiseth him.

Proverbs 14:16

A wise man feareth, and departeth from evil: but the fool rageth, and is confident.

Proverbs 14:26

In the fear of the Lord is strong confidence: and his children shall have a place of refuge.

Proverbs 14:27

The fear of the Lord is a fountain of life, to depart from the snares of death.

Proverbs 15:16
Better is little with the fear of the Lord than great treasure and trouble therewith.

Proverbs 15:33
The fear of the Lord is the instruction of wisdom; and before honour is humility.

Proverbs 16:6
By mercy and truth iniquity is purged: and by the fear of the Lord men depart from evil.

Proverbs 19:23
The fear of the Lord tendeth to life: and he that hath it shall abide satisfied; he shall not be visited with evil.

Proverbs 22:4
By humility and the fear of the Lord are riches, and honour, and life.

Proverbs 23:17
Let not thine heart envy sinners: but be thou in the fear of the Lord all the day long.

Proverbs 29:25
The fear of man bringeth a snare: but whoso putteth his trust in the Lord shall be safe.

Proverbs 31:30
Favour is deceitful, and beauty is vain: but a woman that feareth the Lord, she shall be praised.

Ecclesiastes 8:12

Though a sinner do evil an hundred times, and his days be prolonged, yet surely I know that it shall be well with them that fear God, which fear before him:

Ecclesiastes 8:13

But it shall not be well with the wicked, neither shall he prolong his days, which are as a shadow; because he feareth not before God.

Ecclesiastes 9:2

All things come alike to all: there is one event to the righteous, and to the wicked; to the good and to the clean, and to the unclean; to him that sacrificeth, and to him that sacrificeth not: as is the good, so is the sinner; and he that sweareth, as he that feareth an oath.

Isaiah 8:12

Say ye not, A confederacy, to all them to whom this people shall say, A confederacy; neither fear ye their fear, nor be afraid

Isaiah 35:4

Say to them that are of a fearful heart, Be strong, fear not: behold, your God will come with vengeance, even God with a recompence; he will come and save you

Isaiah 41:10

Fear thou not; for I am with thee: be not dismayed; for I am thy God: I will strengthen thee; yea, I will help thee; yea, I will uphold thee with the right hand of my righteousness.

Isaiah 41:13

For I the Lord thy God will hold thy right hand, saying unto thee, Fear not; I will help thee.

Isaiah 41:14

Fear not, thou worm Jacob, and ye men of Israel; I will help thee, saith the Lord, and thy redeemer, the Holy One of Israel.

Isaiah 43:1

But now thus saith the Lord that created thee, O Jacob, and he that formed thee, O Israel, Fear not: for I have redeemed thee, I have called thee by thy name; thou art mine.

Isaiah 43:5

Fear not: for I am with thee: I will bring thy seed from the east, and gather thee from the west;

Isaiah 44:2

Thus saith the Lord that made thee, and formed thee from the womb, which will help thee; Fear not, O Jacob, my servant; and thou, Jesurun, whom I have chosen.

Isaiah 44:8

Fear ye not, neither be afraid: have not I told thee from that time, and have declared it? ye are even my witnesses. Is there a God beside me? yea, there is no God; I know not any.

Isaiah 44:11

Behold, all his fellows shall be ashamed: and the workmen, they are of men: let them all be gathered together, let them stand up; yet they shall fear, and they shall be ashamed together.

Isaiah 50:10

Who is among you that feareth the Lord, that obeyeth the voice of his servant, that walketh in darkness, and hath no light? let him trust in the name of the Lord, and stay upon his God.

Isaiah 51:7

Hearken unto me, ye that know righteousness, the people in whose heart is my law; fear ye not the reproach of men, neither be ye afraid of their revilings.

Isaiah 51:13

And forgettest the Lord thy maker, that hath stretched forth the heavens, and laid the foundations of the earth; and hast feared continually every day because of the fury of the oppressor, as if he were ready to destroy? and where is the fury of the oppressor?

Isaiah 54:4

Fear not; for thou shalt not be ashamed: neither be thou confounded; for thou shalt not be put to shame: for thou shalt forget the shame of thy youth, and shalt not remember the reproach of thy widowhood any more.

Isaiah 54:14

In righteousness shalt thou be established: thou shalt be far from oppression; for thou shalt not fear: and from terror; for it shall not come near thee.

Isaiah 59:19

So shall they fear the name of the Lord from the west, and his glory from the rising of the sun. When the enemy shall come in like a flood, the Spirit of the Lord shall lift up a standard against him.

Isaiah 60:5

Then thou shalt see, and flow together, and thine heart shall fear, and be enlarged; because the abundance of the sea shall be converted unto thee, the forces of the Gentiles shall come unto thee.

Amos 3:8

The lion hath roared, who will not fear? the Lord God hath spoken, who can but prophesy

Malachi 3:5

And I will come near to you to judgment; and I will be a swift witness against the sorcerers, and against the adulterers, and against false swearers, and against those that oppress the hireling in his wages, the widow, and the fatherless, and that turn aside the stranger from his right, and fear not me, saith the Lord of hosts.

Malachi 4:2

But unto you that fear my name shall the Sun of righteousness arise with healing in his wings; and ye shall go forth, and grow up as calves of the stall

Matthew 8:26

And he saith unto them, Why are ye fearful, O ye of little faith? Then he arose, and rebuked the winds and the sea; and there was a great calm.

Matthew 10:26

Fear them not therefore: for there is nothing covered, that shall not be revealed; and hid, that shall not be known.

Matthew 10:28

And fear not them which kill the body, but are not able to kill the soul: but rather fear him which is able to destroy both soul and body in hell.

Matthew 10:31

Fear ye not therefore, ye are of more value than many sparrows.

Matthew 27:54

Now when the centurion, and they that were with him, watching Jesus, saw the earthquake, and those things that were done, they feared greatly, saying, Truly this was the Son of God.

Matthew 28:4

And for fear of him the keepers did shake, and became as dead men.

Matthew 28:5

And the angel answered and said unto the women, Fear not ye: for I know that ye seek Jesus, which was crucified.

Matthew 28:8

And they departed quickly from the sepulchre with fear and great joy; and did run to bring his disciples word.

Mark 4:40

And he said unto them, Why are ye so fearful? how is it that ye have no faith?

Mark 4:41

And they feared exceedingly, and said one to another, What manner of man is this, that even the wind and the sea obey him?

Luke 1:50

And his mercy is on them that fear him from generation to generation

Luke 1:74

That he would grant unto us, that we being delivered out of the hand of our enemies might serve him without fear,

In Context | Full Chapter | Other Translations

Luke 2:10

And the angel said unto them, Fear not: for, behold, I bring you good tidings of great joy, which shall be to all people.

Luke 1:74

That he would grant unto us, that we being delivered out of the hand of our enemies might serve him without fear,

Luke 2:10

And the angel said unto them, Fear not: for, behold, I bring you good tidings of great joy, which shall be to all people

.Luke 8:50

But when Jesus heard it, he answered him, saying, Fear not: believe only, and she shall be made whole.

Luke 12:5

But I will forewarn you whom ye shall fear: Fear him, which after he hath killed hath power to cast into hell; yea, I say unto you, Fear him.

Luke 12:7

But even the very hairs of your head are all numbered. Fear not therefore: ye are of more value than many sparrows.

Luke 12:32

Fear not, little flock; for it is your Father's good pleasure to give you the kingdom.

Acts 2:43

And fear came upon every soul: and many wonders and signs were done by the apostles

Acts 9:31

Then had the churches rest throughout all Judaea and Galilee and Samaria, and were edified; and walking in the fear of the Lord, and in the comfort of the Holy Ghost, were multiplied

Romans 8:15

For ye have not received the spirit of bondage again to fear; but ye have received the Spirit of adoption, whereby we cry, Abba, Father.

Wherefore, my beloved, as ye have always obeyed, not as in my presence only, but now much more in my absence, work out your own salvation with fear and trembling.

2 Timothy 1:7

For God hath not given us the spirit of fear; but of power, and of love, and of a sound mind.

Hebrews 2:15

And deliver them who through fear of death were all their lifetime subject to bondage.

Hebrews 10:31

It is a fearful thing to fall into the hands of the living God

Hebrews 13:6

So that we may boldly say, The Lord is my helper, and I will not fear what man shall do unto me.

1 Peter 3:15

But sanctify the Lord God in your hearts: and be ready always to give an answer to every man that asketh you a reason of the hope that is in you with meekness and fear:

1 John 4:18

There is no fear in love; but perfect love casteth out fear: because fear hath torment. He that feareth is not made perfect in love.

Jude 1:23

And others save with fear, pulling them out of the fire; hating even the garment spotted by the flesh.

Revelation 1:17

And when I saw him, I fell at his feet as dead. And he laid his right hand upon me, saying unto me, Fear not; I am the first and the last:

Revelation 2:10

Fear none of those things which thou shalt suffer: behold, the devil shall cast some of you into prison, that ye may be tried; and ye shall have tribulation ten days: be thou faithful unto death, and I will give thee a crown of life.

Revelation 11:11

And after three days and an half the spirit of life from God entered into them, and they stood upon their feet; and great fear fell upon them which saw them.

Revelation 11:18

And the nations were angry, and thy wrath is come, and the time of the dead, that they should be judged, and that thou shouldest give reward unto thy servants the prophets, and to the saints, and them that fear thy name, small and great; and shouldest destroy them which destroy the earth.

Revelation 14:7

Saying with a loud voice, Fear God, and give glory to him; for the hour of his judgment is come: and worship him that made heaven, and earth, and the sea, and the fountains of waters.

Revelation 15:4

Who shall not fear thee, O Lord, and glorify thy name? for thou only art holy: for all nations shall come and worship before thee; for thy judgments are made manifest.

Revelation 21:8

But the fearful, and unbelieving, and the abominable, and murderers, and whoremongers, and sorcerers, and idolaters, and all liars, shall have their part in the lake which burneth with fire and brimstone: which is the second death.

# 19

# About the Author

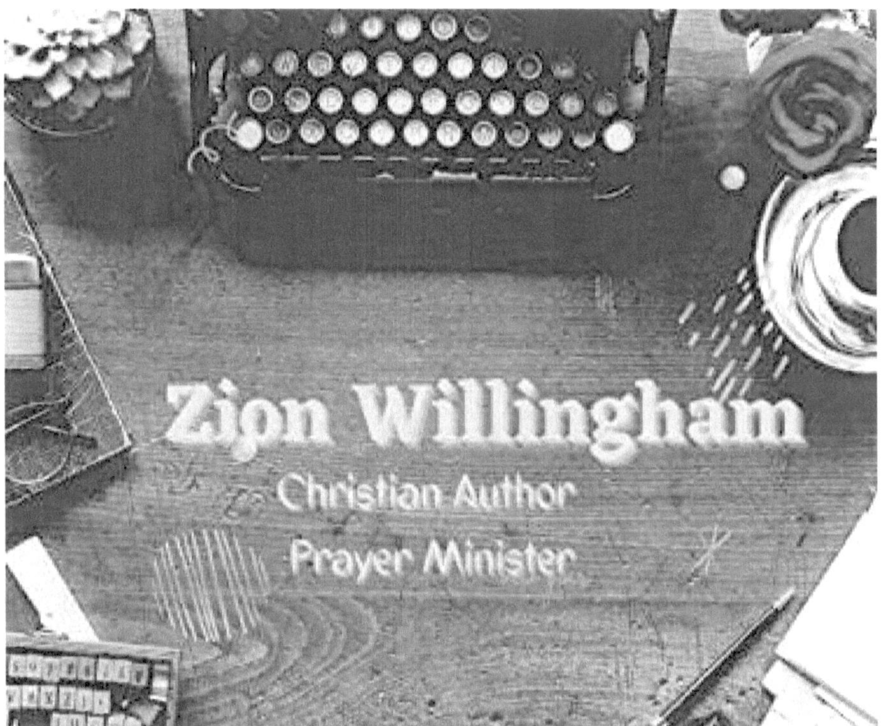

Zion Willingham is the author of Trigger Warning, Natural Health and Divine Healing, Take Your Life Back from Familiar Spirits, and the Battle Plan series.

She has a unique focus on prayer with special attention to individuals with deep soul wounds and abuse.

Zion is also the prophetic voice behind Sanctuary Prayer Ministries. Sanctuary Prayer Ministries is a ministry that exists with the sole purpose of seeking God in prayer and fulfilling the great mandate.

We only have one agenda, and that is to pray and study the Word of God. Books written by Zion Willingham are available on all of the major ebook resellers.

Join us for a weekly message on our website directly at https://prayerpurpose. online.church/ In addition, we invite you to visit our podcast and fellowship with us at https://tinyurl.com/SanctuaryPodcasts
https://parentsarms.com
https://zionwillingham.com/home-2